*Especially for*

Miriam

*From*

Your Merrill Family

*Date*

2.9.20

# Everyday Inspiration from Psalm 23

## A Devotional Journal for Women

BARBOUR BOOKS

An Imprint of Barbour Publishing, Inc.

Published by Barbour Books, an imprint of Barbour Publishing, Inc., 1810 Barbour Drive, Uhrichsville, Ohio 44683, www.barbourbooks.com

*Our mission is to inspire the world with the life-changing message of the Bible.*

Member of the
Evangelical Christian
Publishers Association

Printed in China.

# Contents

Introduction . . . . . . . . . . . . . . . . . . . . . . . . . . . . . . . . 7

1. Belonging to Him . . . . . . . . . . . . . . . . . . . . . . . . 9

2. From His Hand . . . . . . . . . . . . . . . . . . . . . . . . . 21

3. In His Presence . . . . . . . . . . . . . . . . . . . . . . . . 33

4. Breathe In . . . . . . . . . . . . . . . . . . . . . . . . . . . . 45

5. God's Goodness . . . . . . . . . . . . . . . . . . . . . . . . 57

6. Whatever Our Needs . . . . . . . . . . . . . . . . . . . . 69

7. Take Heart . . . . . . . . . . . . . . . . . . . . . . . . . . . . 81

8. Following Him . . . . . . . . . . . . . . . . . . . . . . . . . 95

9. Protecting His Own . . . . . . . . . . . . . . . . . . . . 107

10. In the Midst . . . . . . . . . . . . . . . . . . . . . . . . . .121

11. Home at Last . . . . . . . . . . . . . . . . . . . . . . . . . 133

12. In His Service . . . . . . . . . . . . . . . . . . . . . . . . 145

13. Blessed . . . . . . . . . . . . . . . . . . . . . . . . . . . . . .157

14. Be Happy . . . . . . . . . . . . . . . . . . . . . . . . . . . . 169

15. All in All . . . . . . . . . . . . . . . . . . . . . . . . . . . . .181

# Introduction

The twenty-third Psalm is one of the most memorized and used sections of scripture in the Bible. Its words are spoken by a broken man to an all-loving God in praise and supplication. The writer, David, was a shepherd, so his word pictures are painted from his experiences. He rested in the green pastures, he walked through the dark valleys, and all along he knew of God's faithfulness. David might have written these words while he was on the same field where the angels announced Christ's birth. What a time of joy!

Psalm 23 is called a psalm of confidence, so trust that the Lord knows your heart and will hear you and be merciful. As you journey through these pages, let the words wash over you. Drink in the depths of each phrase and hear melodies of love and the promise of the Good Shepherd's care.

# Belonging to Him

# In the Fold

---

*The LORD is my shepherd.*
PSALM 23:1 NIV

What a comfort the first line of Psalm 23 is to believers when we realize what care a shepherd takes of his sheep. David was a young shepherd when the Lord first tapped him for service. At that time, he worked on a hillside caring for his family's flock. The sheep—though smelly, often unruly, and not quite smart—were his responsibility. David knew when the animals needed food and water; he kept them safe from predators. He was their provider and protector. It follows, then, when he penned the first line of this psalm, he recognized the job description.

Our God is our Shepherd when we choose to let Him guide us. As a wayward lamb can flee from the flock, we must safeguard our hearts and stay in the fold. Not follow the crowd, but follow the Shepherd: the One who will never leave us alone or unprotected. The beauty of having a shepherd is realizing He is our ally and strength, our Guide. Just as David wouldn't lead his lambs into danger, our Lord will do the same. His desire is for our obedience. He is our safety and refuge. Draw near to the Good Shepherd this day.

*Like a shepherd, he will care
for his flock, gathering the
lambs in his arms, hugging
them as he carries them.*

ISAIAH 40:11 MSG

---

*"'But you, Bethlehem, in the land
of Judah, are by no means least
among the rulers of Judah; for out
of you will come a ruler who will
shepherd my people Israel.'"*

MATTHEW 2:6 NIV

---

*When Jesus landed and saw a
large crowd, he had compassion on
them, because they were like sheep
without a shepherd. So he began
teaching them many things.*

MARK 6:34 NIV

The sweetest word of the whole
is that monosyllable, *"My."*
He does not say, "The Lord is the
shepherd of the world at large,
and leadeth forth the multitude
as his flock," but "The Lord is *my*
shepherd"; if he be a Shepherd to
no one else, he is a Shepherd
to *me;* he cares for *me,* watches
over *me,* and preserves *me.*
The words are in the present tense.

CHARLES SPURGEON

Men spontaneously praise
whatever they value.

C. S. LEWIS

*The LORD is my shepherd,*
*I lack nothing.*
PSALM 23:1 NIV

When it comes to brains, sheep are not the brightest crayons in the box. They frighten easily, tend to follow the crowd, and have limited abilities for defending themselves. That's why sheep thrive best with a shepherd who guides, protects, and cares for their needs. Our Good Shepherd will do the same for us. Worry, fear, and discontent are products of a sheepish mentality. However, the peace of true contentment can be ours when we follow God's lead.

# My Shepherd

---

Dearest Lord, I want to thank You for Your hand of protection
even when I don't recognize what You are doing in my life. With my
whole heart, I praise You for Your steadfastness and goodness, Your love
and mercy. You are the Everlasting God. Please guide me through life
and keep me by Your side. Let me feel Your heartbeat. I choose
You as my Shepherd and desire to stay in Your fold. Amen.

*Now may the God of peace,
who through the blood of the eternal
covenant brought back from the dead our
Lord Jesus, that great Shepherd of the
sheep, equip you with everything good for
doing his will, and may he work in
us what is pleasing to him, through
Jesus Christ, to whom be glory
for ever and ever. Amen.*

HEBREWS 13:20–21 NIV

---

*Once you were like sheep who
wandered away. But now you
have turned to your Shepherd,
the Guardian of your souls.*

1 PETER 2:25 NLT

*And when the Chief Shepherd appears,*
*you will receive the crown of glory*
*that will never fade away.*

1 Peter 5:4 niv

---

*"I am the Good Shepherd. The Good*
*Shepherd puts the sheep before himself,*
*sacrifices himself if necessary. A hired*
*man is not a real shepherd. The sheep*
*mean nothing to him. He sees a wolf*
*come and runs for it, leaving the sheep*
*to be ravaged and scattered by the wolf.*
*He's only in it for the money.*
*The sheep don't matter to him."*

John 10:11–13 msg

*You are my hiding place; you will
protect me from trouble and surround
me with songs of deliverance.*

PSALM 32:7 NIV

---

Having an alarm system installed in your home can give you a sense of security. If someone tries to break in, you can trust that help is immediately on the way. God is a 24-hour security system. When you call, He's there. But the truth is, God's there even before you call. He won't hesitate to step in to protect you, even if you're unaware of the danger you're in.

# I Will Follow

Father God, I am so thankful I can trust in You to always be
by my side. You are my Shepherd, my leader. You are my strength
and support at all times. As the shepherd hears his sheep when they
bleat, Your ear is tuned to me. When I cry, You hear me. I want
to stay in Your fold, in Your mighty hands. Amen.

Your path with its unexplained
sorrow or turmoil, and mine with
its sharp flints and briers—and both
our paths, with their unexplained
perplexity, their sheer mystery—
they are His paths, on which He will
show Himself loving and faithful.
Nothing else; nothing less.

AMY CARMICHAEL

Where does your security lie?
Is God your refuge, your hiding
place, your stronghold, your shepherd,
your counselor, your friend, your
redeemer, your savior, your guide?
If He is, you don't need to search
any further for security.

ELISABETH ELLIOT

From
His Hand

# The Shepherd Host

*He lets me rest in green meadows;*
*he leads me beside peaceful streams.*
PSALM 23:2 NLT

*I*n our fast-paced world, we often find ourselves overwhelmed with to-do lists and little time to accomplish anything. Fast food, freeways, and frenzy frequent our daily lives. David's words of refreshment in Psalm 23 can serve as a balm to the frazzled. Who wouldn't love the provision of "fresh pastures" and "restful waters"? Even the words convey a sense of calm to the reader. In this simple sentence, we see the God of the universe as a kindly host: One who provides for our needs with a special tenderness and love.

Meditating on these words and knowing for sure that our Jesus wants to supply our needs and allow us rest affords us a peace like no other. Yes, there are tasks at hand for each of us, but we need to remember the times of refreshment and relaxation so we might be reenergized for whatever lies ahead—knowing full well He holds the future. Take a moment to relax. Don't fret over lost time. Be still beside the still waters. Allow yourself time, and enjoy God's presence. Sit in silence and listen for the voice of your Host and allow the rejuvenation of His Spirit within you.

*My sheep listen to my voice;*
*I know them, and they follow me.*

JOHN 10:27 NLT

———◆———

*A Message from Israel's GOD-of-the-Angel-Armies: "When I've turned everything around and brought my people back, the old expressions will be heard on the streets: 'GOD bless you!' . . . 'O True Home!' . . . 'O Holy Mountain!' All Judah's people, whether in town or country, will get along just fine with each other. I'll refresh tired bodies; I'll restore tired souls."*

JEREMIAH 31:23–25 MSG

———◆———

*Then, because so many people were coming and going that they did not even have a chance to eat, he said to them, "Come with me by yourselves to a quiet place and get some rest."*

MARK 6:31 NIV

Psalm 23 is no sundial recording only
sunny hours; it faces faithfully the
dark defile and the lurking foes. At the
same time it honestly and thankfully
remembers life's delights. In short,
it sees life steadily and sees it whole.

THE INTERPRETER'S BIBLE

The branch of the vine does not
worry, and toil, and rush here to
seek for sunshine, and there to
find rain. No; it rests in union and
communion with the vine; and at
the right time, and in the right way,
is the right fruit found on it.
Let us so abide in the Lord Jesus.

HUDSON TAYLOR

*Whoever dwells in the shelter of the Most High
will rest in the shadow of the Almighty.*
PSALM 91:1 NIV

---

Picture a hammock in the shade of two leafy trees, swaying gently in the breeze. Now picture yourself nestled there, eyes closed, totally relaxed. This is what it's like to rest in the shadow of the Almighty. Knowing that God holds you tenderly in His hand, offering protection, comfort, and grace, allows you to let go of your fears and concerns. God knows about them all. Rest in the fact that scripture says nothing is impossible with God.

# Refresh Us

Dear heavenly Father, we are weary. We need Your presence to refresh our bodies, souls, and spirits. We have taken on much and the yoke is heavy on our shoulders. Let us sit and concentrate on Your goodness, focusing on Your majesty. Slow our steps and let our hearts beat in unison with Yours. Show us how to unwind and rest. You are so kind to us. Thank You for this respite. Amen.

*But what can I say? He has spoken to me, and he himself has done this. . . . Lord, by such things people live; and my spirit finds life in them too. You restored me to health and let me live.*

ISAIAH 38:15–16 NIV

---

*"Take my yoke upon you and learn from me, for I am gentle and humble in heart, and you will find rest for your souls. For my yoke is easy and my burden is light."*

MATTHEW 11:29–30 NIV

---

*"For I have given rest to the weary and joy to the sorrowing."*

JEREMIAH 31:25 NLT

*You're all I want in heaven! You're all I want on earth! . . . But I'm in the very presence of GOD—oh, how refreshing it is! I've made Lord GOD my home. GOD, I'm telling the world what you do!*

PSALM 73:25–28 MSG

———

*By the seventh day God had finished the work he had been doing; so on the seventh day he rested from all his work. Then God blessed the seventh day and made it holy, because on it he rested from all the work of creating that he had done.*

GENESIS 2:2–3 NIV

*He makes me lie down in green
pastures, he leads me beside quiet
waters, he refreshes my soul.*
PSALM 23:2–3 NIV

---

*G*od created the world in six days. Then He took a day to sit back and enjoy all of the good things He'd done. The Bible tells us God doesn't tire or sleep, but even He knew the value of a time-out. If you're weary, or simply trying to keep up with a hectic schedule, let God lead you beside quiet waters. Look back over what you and God have accomplished together. Rejoice, then rest so God can restore your spirit.

# After Our Wait

Father God, refresh our spirits with Yours. Like rain falling upon a parched ground, we will drink in the Holy Spirit and listen for Your voice. Pulse through us and fill our souls with Your goodness so we might march forth from this stillness on a journey that You have chosen for us. Thank You for Your gentleness with us each day. Amen.

The freshness of heart in Christ was always the same. You and I get so weary in our experience of the wilderness, but Christ's heart is never wearied, it is as freshly set on the bride as when God chose us in Him before the foundation of the world.

G. V. WIGRAM

Christ's invitation to the weary and heavy-laden is a call to begin life over again upon a new principle—upon His own principle. "Watch My way of doing things," He says. "Follow Me. Take life as I take it. Be meek and lowly, and you will find rest."

HENRY DRUMMOND

# In His Presence

# Let's Roll

*Even when the way goes through Death Valley,*
*I'm not afraid when you walk at my side.*
PSALM 23:4 MSG

The United States changed forever on September 11, 2001, after terrorists attacked our country. Security seemed fleeting. The constants on which we relied shifted. A sense of unease permeated the land.

During the attack, the passengers on board United Airlines Flight 93 discovered their plane had been hijacked and was headed toward the Pentagon. One passenger, Todd Beamer, made a phone call and reached a GTE supervisor, Lisa Jefferson. According to her accounts, a group of people made the decision to fly the plane into the ground before they would allow the hijackers to succeed in their nefarious plan. Beamer calmly recited Psalm 23 with Jefferson before his infamous words, "Are you guys ready? Let's roll."

Faced with certain death, Beamer recognized the significance of David's words to the Lord. Even though I'm going to die, I know You are at my side. *Even though.* False bravado? Not when a believer has hold of the hand of God and can feel His presence.

Death is a certainty—be it today or many years ahead. And our Lord has given His words of promise, that He will be ever present, no matter the circumstances. Believe this day He has you in the palm of His hand and will never let go.

*I declare to you, brothers and sisters, that flesh and blood cannot inherit the kingdom of God, nor does the perishable inherit the imperishable. Listen, I tell you a mystery: We will not all sleep, but we will all be changed—in a flash, in the twinkling of an eye, at the last trumpet. For the trumpet will sound, the dead will be raised imperishable, and we will be changed.*

1 Corinthians 15:50–52 niv

---

*I write these things to you who believe in the name of the Son of God so that you may know that you have eternal life.*

1 John 5:13 niv

He whose head is in heaven need not fear to put his feet into the grave.

MATTHEW HENRY

———•◦•———

We must learn to live on the heavenly side and look at things from above. To contemplate all things as God sees them, as Christ beholds them. . . separates us from the world and conquers fear of death.

A. B. SIMPSON

———•◦•———

Live in Christ, die in Christ, and the flesh need not fear death.

JOHN KNOX

*I'll bless you every day,*
*and keep it up from now to eternity.*
PSALM 145:2 MSG

---

E ternal life isn't a reward we can earn. It's a free gift given by a Father who wants to spend eternity with the children He loves. This gift may be free to us, but it was purchased at a high price. Jesus purchased our lives at the cost of His own. His death on the cross is the bridge that leads us from this life into the next. Forever isn't long enough to say thank You for a gift like that.

# In Times of Grief

Father God, how we need to cling to Your hand in desperate times when overwhelming grief can distort our vision of You and Your goodness. A barrage of questions might begin: *Why? What now?* It's at these times, Lord, we need to lean on You. Make Your presence known so we might realize You love us and we are in Your care that we need not fear. Thank You, Lord. Amen.

*May the God of hope fill you with all joy and peace as you trust in him, so that you may overflow with hope by the power of the Holy Spirit.*

ROMANS 15:13 NIV

---

*As for me, I look to the LORD for help. I wait confidently for God to save me, and my God will certainly hear me.*

MICAH 7:7 NLT

---

*GOD makes his people strong. GOD gives his people peace.*

PSALM 29:11 MSG

---

*For we live by faith, not by sight.*

2 CORINTHIANS 5:7 NIV

"And you, my child, [Jesus] will be called a prophet of the Most High. . . to shine on those living in darkness and in the shadow of death, to guide our feet into the path of peace."

LUKE 1:76, 79 NIV

---

"I'm telling you these things while I'm still living with you. The Friend, the Holy Spirit whom the Father will send at my request, will make everything plain to you. He will remind you of all the things I have told you. I'm leaving you well and whole. That's my parting gift to you. Peace. I don't leave you the way you're used to being left—feeling abandoned, bereft. So don't be upset. Don't be distraught."

JOHN 14:25–27 MSG

*I cry to God to help me. From his palace*
*he hears my call; my cry brings me right*
*into his presence—a private audience!*
PSALM 18:6 MSG

---

*I*t can be difficult to picture yourself in the presence of someone you cannot see. But the Bible assures us God is near. His Spirit not only surrounds us, but moves within us. When God's presence feels far away, remember that what you feel is not an accurate gauge of the truth. Read the Psalms to remind yourself that others have felt the way you do. Then, follow the psalmists' example. Continue praising God and moving ahead in faith.

# In Your Arms

Dear Lord, thank You for Your ever-present kindness and mercy. Wrap Your arms about us so we might feel Your heavenly touch. We love You and want to walk in the way You would have us go. When our gaze wavers, help us fix our eyes upon You. If You are for us, then who could be against us? Even though we walk through the valley, we know there is a mountaintop waiting. Amen.

The man or woman who is wholly or joyously surrendered to Christ can't make a wrong choice—any choice will be the right one.

A. W. TOZER

––––•––––

When it seems as if God is far away, remind yourself that He is near. Nearness is not a matter of geography. God is everywhere. Nearness is likeness. The more we become like the Lord, the nearer He is to us.

WARREN WIERSBE

––––•––––

Let this encourage those of you who belong to Christ: the storm may be tempestuous, but it is only temporary. The clouds that are temporarily rolling over your head will pass, and then you will have fair weather, an eternal sunshine of glory.

WILLIAM GURNALL

Breathe In

# A Respite

*True to your word, you let me catch my*
*breath and send me in the right direction.*
PSALM 23:3 MSG

We all have times in our lives when we feel we can't catch our breath. The next "thing" demands we move on. The next worry consumes our thoughts. Anxiety creeps in and we focus only on the negative. This happens most often when we are exhausted. We've run out of steam.

Don't you think David felt this way when he penned the Psalms? He was on the run for his life. An enemy behind every rock could swoop in at any time. Yet he knew to keep his eyes focused on the Lord. True to God's Word: he knew of God's faithfulness, God's provision, God's care, and he trusted. He trusted enough to stop running and rest, physically and emotionally.

Emotional distress can wrap its tentacles around us so tightly we aren't able to breathe. It's at these times when we must lift our eyes to God and know His mercies are forever. Take a deep breath and breathe in His goodness. Feel the air whoosh inside your lungs and release it slowly. The Holy Spirit will draw you near and give you comfort in times of distress to provide you rest, a respite, a reprieve. Just breathe.

*Do you not know? Have you not heard?*
*The LORD is the everlasting God,*
*the Creator of the ends of the earth.*
*He will not grow tired or weary, and his*
*understanding no one can fathom.*

ISAIAH 40:28 NIV

---

*You gave abundant showers, O God;*
*you refreshed your weary inheritance.*
*Your people settled in it, and from*
*your bounty, God, you provided.*

PSALM 68:9–10 NIV

---

*Even youths grow tired and weary, and*
*young men stumble and fall; but those*
*who hope in the LORD will renew their*
*strength. They will soar on wings like*
*eagles; they will run and not grow weary,*
*they will walk and not be faint.*

ISAIAH 40:30–31 NIV

We can be tired, weary, and
emotionally distraught, but after
spending time alone with God,
we find that He injects into our
bodies energy, power, and strength.

CHARLES STANLEY

Are you weak? Weary? Confused?
Troubled? Pressured? How is your
relationship with God? Is it held in its
place of priority? I believe the greater
the pressure, the greater your need
for time alone with Him.

KAY ARTHUR

*Praise be to the Lord, to God our*
*Savior, who daily bears our burdens.*
PSALM 68:19 NIV

ome things are too heavy to carry alone. A couch, for instance. Or a washing machine. The same is true for the mental and emotional burdens we bear. The good news is that strength, peace, comfort, hope, and a host of other helping hands are only a prayer away. We're never alone in our pain or struggle. God is always near, right beside us, ready to help carry what's weighing us down.

# Reaching High

Father Most High, thank You for Your love and care. We make a choice to rest our heads upon Your breast and hear Your heartbeat, in turn slowing ours. Tangled in the cares of the day, we tire easily and need support. Your Word promises to give us what we need, so we reach our hands to You and ask. Bless Your holy name. Amen.

*Then we will not turn away from you;*
*revive us, and we will call on your name.*
PSALM 80:18 NIV

---

*"I'll make a covenant of peace with*
*them. I'll banish fierce animals from*
*the country so the sheep can live safely*
*in the wilderness and sleep in the forest.*
*I'll make them and everything around*
*my hill a blessing. I'll send down plenty*
*of rain in season—showers of blessing!*
*The trees in the orchards will bear fruit,*
*the ground will produce, they'll feel*
*content and safe on their land, and*
*they'll realize that I am GOD."*
EZEKIEL 34:25–27 MSG

---

*Come near to God and he*
*will come near to you.*
JAMES 4:8 NIV

*"So I say to you: Ask and it will be given
to you; seek and you will find; knock
and the door will be opened to you.
For everyone who asks receives; the one
who seeks finds; and to the one who
knocks, the door will be opened."*

LUKE 11:9–10 NIV

———◦———

*Praise be to the Lord, to God our
Savior, who daily bears our burdens.
Our God is a God who saves.*

PSALM 68:19–20 NIV

*Cast your burden on the LORD,*
*and He shall sustain you; He shall*
*never permit the righteous to be moved.*
PSALM 55:22 NKJV

---

*C*asting a fishing line is an almost effortless motion. Casting a burden paints a totally different image. Burdens are pictured as heavy, cumbersome, not easily carried—let alone "cast." But casting our burdens on God is as easy as speaking to Him in prayer. It's calling for help when we need it, admitting our sin when we've fallen, and letting our tears speak for our hearts when words fail us.

# Knowing You Are There

Father God, how we bless Your holy name. We turn to You this day when circumstances have tied us in knots; yet despite the turmoil, we know You are at work in our lives. Help us trust You even when we don't feel like it. Lead us to a place where we might catch our breath. Thank You for Your Holy Spirit, the Comforter, who will always help us find rest. Amen.

To every toiling, heavy-laden sinner, Jesus says, "Come to me and rest." But there are many toiling, heavy-laden believers, too. For them this same invitation is meant. Note well the words of Jesus, if you are heavy-laden with your service, and do not mistake it. It is not, "Go, labor on," as perhaps you imagine. On the contrary, it is "stop, turn back, come to me and rest." Never, never did Christ send a heavy laden one to work; never, never did He send a hungry one, a weary one, a sick or sorrowing one, away on any service. For such the Bible only says, "Come, come, come."

HUDSON TAYLOR

God's Goodness

# No Matter What

*Surely your goodness and unfailing
love will pursue me all the days of my life.*
PSALM 23:6 NLT

The psalmist's statement "will pursue me all the days of my life" suggests a continuing on the journey with the shepherd. He has watched over his flock, fed and protected it. Nothing has escaped the eye of the shepherd. If he looks behind him, he will not see an enemy, *only* God's gifts of goodness and mercy. The sheep can stake their lives on their shepherd's faithfulness. We are not always faithful. We stumble and forget or ignore what we know to be right. Yet our good God cares for us. No matter what, we cannot fall from the hand of our Lord, our Shepherd. He has a grip on us and will never let go. Even when our fingers slacken, His grasp does not. Through personal experience we can feel His care when we surrender to Him. Then when we look over our shoulder at the past, we can see His merciful hand at work.

God looks at us spirit to spirit, which is the part of us that is beyond reproach. How good of God! How merciful, for we do fall short. Yet our loving heavenly Father looks at us through His holiness with eyes of love. No matter what.

*His divine power has given us everything we need for a godly life through our knowledge of him who called us by his own glory and goodness.*

2 PETER 1:3 NIV

---

*I will make an everlasting covenant with them: I will never stop doing good to them.*

JEREMIAH 32:40 NIV

---

*"If you then, though you are evil, know how to give good gifts to your children, how much more will your Father in heaven give the Holy Spirit to those who ask him!"*

LUKE 11:13 NIV

O God, Thou art a Spirit, infinite, eternal, and unchangeable in Thy being, wisdom, power, holiness, justice, goodness, and truth.

GEORGE GILLESPIE

---

The [psalmist] has found the guide leads wisely and leads well; wherefore he has confidence in the future.

THE INTERPRETER'S BIBLE

---

I believe the Bible is the best gift God has ever given to man. All the good from the Savior of the world is communicated to us through this book.

ABRAHAM LINCOLN

*I would have lost heart, unless I had*
*believed that I would see the goodness*
*of the* LORD *in the land of the living.*

PSALM 27:13 NKJV

———◦◦◦———

Knowing a friend's heart toward you can help you relax and be yourself. With a friend like this, you can honestly share your deepest secrets, feelings, and failures without fear of ridicule or reprisal. The psalms remind us over and over again that God's heart toward us is good. Believing in God's innate goodness means we can entrust every detail of our lives to Him without hesitation.

# Wandering Sheep

All Good and Knowing God, how we thank You for Your faithfulness.
Though we stray from Your paths, You allow us to repent and return.
Day after day we learn more of Your wonderful love for us. It's amazing.
"I once was lost but now am found." What wonderful words of affirmation
that remind us of a loving Jesus. Bless You, Lord. Amen.

*Jesus said, "I am the Bread of Life. The person who aligns with me hungers no more and thirsts no more, ever. I have told you this explicitly because even though you have seen me in action, you don't really believe me. Every person the Father gives me eventually comes running to me. And once that person is with me, I hold on and don't let go. I came down from heaven not to follow my own whim but to accomplish the will of the One who sent me."*

JOHN 6:35–38 MSG

---

*So I live in this earthly body by trusting in the Son of God, who loved me and gave himself for me.*

GALATIANS 2:20 NLT

> *In him we have redemption through his blood, the forgiveness of sins, in accordance with the riches of God's grace that he lavished on us. With all wisdom and understanding, he made known to us the mystery of his will according to his good pleasure, which he purposed in Christ.*
>
> EPHESIANS 1:7–9 NIV

*The LORD is good. His unfailing love*
*continues forever, and his faithfulness*
*continues to each generation.*
PSALM 100:5 NLT

———————————

With time, we come to believe certain things are unshakable. The sun rises and sets. The tides ebb and flow. Seasons revolve year after year. Babies are born, people die, and the world goes on pretty much as it has for centuries: faithful to a predictable pattern. But there will come a time when the world as we know it will end. Only God is totally unshakable and unchanging. His love and goodness to us will remain forever faithful.

# Our Trust

---

Dear Lord, our hearts are full of gratitude for Your unwavering love and mercies, which are new every day. You are our strength as we lean on You and learn from Your Word. Keep us in the palm of Your hand, Father, lest we slip and be destroyed. Bless us from the wellspring of Your affection and hold us fast. Amen.

Receive every day as a resurrection from death, as a new enjoyment of life; meet every rising sun with such sentiments of God's goodness, as if you had seen it, and all things, new-created upon your account: and under the sense of so great a blessing, let your joyful heart praise and magnify so good and glorious a Creator.

WILLIAM LAW

God's mercy with a sinner is only equaled and perhaps outmatched by His patience with the saints, with you and me.

ALAN REDPATH

Whatever
Our Needs

# Needing or Wanting

*God, my shepherd! I don't need a thing.*
PSALM 23:1 MSG

The Wants vs. The Needs. We seem to have this battle daily. And at times, it's hard to recognize the difference. We want the best for our lives, our families. That's a legitimate thought. However, what we want might not always be what we need. It's wonderful that our God is in the business of helping us make the right choices, when we listen.

When God is truly our Shepherd, guiding and directing, and we are obedient sheep who listen for His call, the Holy Spirit will help us discern the differences. The psalmist tells us God promises to provide for our needs. Paul found this true in his life. He traveled from city to city with no thought of how he'd afford anything. He truly trusted his Shepherd. He was tuned in to the Holy Spirit and ready to step forward in faith.

How easy this sounds. Just believe, and it's going to happen. But our faith wavers. Doubt, maybe panic, seeps in. We are not so sure about things. At these times, it's necessary to open the Bible and soak in His words. We can't assemble our lives because we haven't read the directions! Read and listen. Let Him filter our thoughts and help us make the right decision. Time for: "God? Where are You? I need… Or is it I want…?"

*You can be sure that God will
take care of everything you need,
his generosity exceeding even yours
in the glory that pours from Jesus.
Our God and Father abounds in
glory that just pours out into eternity. Yes.*

PHILIPPIANS 4:19–20 MSG

---

*"Leave here, turn eastward and hide
in the Kerith Ravine, east of the
Jordan. You will drink from the
brook, and I have directed the ravens
to supply you with food there."*

1 KINGS 17:3–5 NIV

---

*Provide them with some animals, plenty
of bread and wine and oil. Load them
with provisions from all the blessings with
which GOD, your God, has blessed you.*

DEUTERONOMY 15:13 MSG

God knows what each one of us is dealing with. He knows our pressures. He knows our conflicts. And He has made a provision for each and every one of them. That provision is Himself in the person of the Holy Spirit, indwelling us and empowering us to respond rightly.

KAY ARTHUR

What we count the ills of life are often blessings in disguise, resulting in good to us in the end. Though for the present not joyous but grievous, yet, if received in a right spirit, they work out fruits of righteousness for us at last.

MATTHEW HENRY

*Each day that we live, he provides for our needs
and gives us the strength of a young eagle.*
PSALM 103:5 CEV

---

What do you need today? Whether it's the finances to pay a fast-approaching bill or the courage to have a difficult conversation with a friend, God wants to provide what you need. Share your heart with Him. But before you rush off to other things, sit quietly and listen. God may reveal how you can work with Him to meet that need. He may also want to help you share with others what He's already so generously provided.

# Our Supplication

Father God, we have so many needs in our lives and we recognize You are not shorthanded. You own the cattle on a thousand hills. Today our hearts speak to You in need. We implore You to fulfill these requests in Your timely manner and ways. Thank You in advance for how You are working in our lives, even when we don't realize it. You are mighty. Amen.

> *"Steep yourself in God-reality, God-initiative, God-provisions. You'll find all your everyday human concerns will be met. Don't be afraid of missing out. You're my dearest friends! The Father wants to give you the very kingdom itself."*
>
> LUKE 12:29–30 MSG

---

> *"Acknowledge the God of your father, and serve him with wholehearted devotion and with a willing mind, for the LORD searches every heart and understands every desire and every thought. If you seek him, he will be found by you; but if you forsake him, he will reject you forever."*
>
> 1 CHRONICLES 28:9 NIV

However many blessings we expect from God, His infinite liberality will always exceed all our wishes and our thoughts.

JOHN CALVIN

⸺•◆•⸺

A thankful heart is one of the primary identifying characteristics of a believer. It stands in stark contrast to pride, selfishness, and worry. And it helps fortify the believer's trust in the Lord and reliance of His provision, even in the toughest times. No matter how choppy the seas become, a believer's heart is buoyed by constant praise and gratefulness to the Lord.

JOHN MACARTHUR

*He covers the heavens with clouds,*
*provides rain for the earth, and makes*
*the grass grow in mountain pastures.*
PSALM 147:8 NLT

---

God provides for us in so many ways that it's easy to take them for granted. The fact that the sun rises each morning, encouraging crops to grow, or that our heart takes its next beat and our lungs their next breath are just a few of the countless gifts we receive from God's almighty hand. As you go through the day, consider the big and little ways God meets your needs. Then take time at day's end to give thanks.

# Our Road Map

Heavenly and Most Merciful God, help us hear You speak to our hearts—go this way and that. Help us learn to trust in You for all we need. It is our desire to walk with You closely, but we falter and misstep. Please hold us by our hands and guide us on the straight and narrow. Day by day, we focus our eyes upon You and wait to see what wondrous things you will do in our lives. Amen.

In the midst of the awesomeness, a touch comes, and you know it is the right hand of Jesus Christ. You know it is not the hand of restraint, correction, nor chastisement, but the right hand of the Everlasting Father. Whenever His hand is laid upon you, it gives inexpressible peace and comfort, and the sense that "underneath are the everlasting arms" (Deuteronomy 33:27), full of support, provision, comfort, and strength.

OSWALD CHAMBERS

---

God knows what each one of us is dealing with. He knows our pressures. He knows our conflicts. And He has made a provision for each and every one of them. That provision is Himself in the person of the Holy Spirit, indwelling us and empowering us to respond rightly.

KAY ARTHUR

# Take Heart

# It's All Right

*I'm not afraid when you walk at my side.*
PSALM 23:4 MSG

---

O God our help in ages past, our hope for years to come. Our shelter from the stormy blast and our eternal home." Words penned by Isaac Watts in the song "O God, Our Help in Ages Past" resonate with our souls. A shelter from the storm. What a comforting word picture.

Storms often assault us: arguments with others, a frightening diagnosis, a financial crisis. Storms come in many forms. They buffet and batter away at our faith. Uncertainty creeps in. Overwhelming questions rise up and barrage us day and night, robbing us of rest. We toss and turn and cry out to God. *How could this happen? Why me? When will it end? What's next?*

Stop. It.

Take heart and know you are a chosen one, and the King of kings is in charge. When you rest in Him and wait, in a still, small voice God speaks, *"Take heart, for I am with you always."* Nothing surprises Him. When we can be still and calm ourselves, the Holy Spirit will minister to our hearts and we will come to realize He does walk by our side.

*"But he brought us out from there to bring us in and give us the land he promised on oath to our ancestors. The LORD commanded us to obey all these decrees and to fear the LORD our God, so that we might always prosper and be kept alive, as is the case today. And if we are careful to obey all this law before the LORD our God, as he has commanded us, that will be our righteousness."*

DEUTERONOMY 6:23–25 NIV

---

*She is clothed with strength and dignity, and she laughs without fear of the future. When she speaks, her words are wise, and she gives instructions with kindness.*

PROVERBS 31:25–26 NLT

Don't be obsessed with getting more material things. Be relaxed with what you have. Since God assured us, "I'll never let you down, never walk off and leave you," we can boldly quote, God is there, ready to help; I'm fearless no matter what. Who or what can get to me?

HEBREWS 13:5–6 MSG

LORD, you know the hopes of the helpless. Surely you will hear their cries and comfort them.

PSALM 10:17 NLT

But God will never forget the needy; the hope of the afflicted will never perish.

PSALM 9:18 NIV

*My heart is confident in you, O God; my heart*
*is confident. No wonder I can sing your praises!*
PSALM 57:7 NLT

———— ◦·◦ ————

*I*n the Bible, when a word or phrase is repeated, it's time to pay attention. In
the original language of the Old Testament, this signifies that something is
the best, the ultimate, the pièce de résistance! The psalmist in Psalm 57 doubly
notes how confident his heart is in God. No wonder praise comes naturally to him!
Take it from the psalmist: you need never doubt God's heart toward you. You can
be confident—eternally confident—in Him.

# Letting Go

Dear Lord, we long to surrender all of our problems and worries to You. Help us to release the tight grip of concern that overwhelms us into Your capable and loving hands. Teach us to trust You for each day and not fret over things that have yet to happen. Still our hearts and minds that we might hear Your voice. Amen.

Doubt discovers difficulties which it never solves; it creates hesitancy, despondency, despair. Its progress is the decay of comfort, the death of peace. "Believe!" is the word which speaks life into a man, but doubt nails down his coffin.

CHARLES SPURGEON

I believe that the happiest of all Christians and the truest of Christians are those who never dare to doubt God, but take His Word simply as it stands, and believe it, and ask no questions, just feeling assured that if God has said it, it will be so.

CHARLES SPURGEON

# Relaxing with You

Father God, thank You for all You have provided for us. Help us to focus on the good and lovely. When our minds race and our hearts rattle our chests, calm us with Your Holy Spirit. We long to keep our focus on You, but our gazes shift and worry creeps in. When we are in doubt, draw us closer to Your breast that we might hear Your heartbeat. Amen.

*But always continue to fear the LORD. You will be rewarded for this; your hope will not be disappointed.*

PROVERBS 23:17–18 NLT

---

*"For I know the plans I have for you," declares the LORD, "plans to prosper you and not to harm you, plans to give you hope and a future."*

JEREMIAH 29:11 NIV

---

*Don't fret or worry. Instead of worrying, pray. Let petitions and praises shape your worries into prayers, letting God know your concerns. Before you know it, a sense of God's wholeness, everything coming together for good, will come and settle you down. It's wonderful what happens when Christ displaces worry at the center of your life.*

PHILIPPIANS 4:6–7 MSG

The lilies grow, Christ says, of
themselves; they toil not, neither
do they spin. They grow, that is,
automatically, spontaneously,
without trying, without
fretting, without thinking.

HENRY DRUMMOND

What I am anxious to see in Christian
believers is a beautiful paradox. I
want to see in them the joy of finding
God while at the same time they are
blessedly pursuing Him. I want to see
in them the great joy of having God,
yet always wanting Him.

A. W. TOZER

*Those who are righteous will be long remembered. They do
not fear bad news; they confidently trust the LORD to care for them.
They are confident and fearless and can face their foes triumphantly.*
PSALM 112:6–8 NLT

We live in uncertain times, economically, politically, and globally. Yet you
can greet each new day with your head held high, confident and unafraid.
Why? Because you have a God who cares deeply about you and the world around
you. When your confidence is placed firmly in God instead of your own abilities,
bank account, or "good karma," you need not fear the future. It's in God's powerful,
capable, and compassionate hands.

# Our Hiding Place

Precious Lord, lead and guide us. Watch over and protect us. We cling to Your right hand and ask for mercy and guidance. Bless and equip us this day with what we need.  Be our shelter from the storm, a cleft in the rock where we might hide. Thank You for sending us Your Son, that we might believe in Him and know this day we walk with You. Amen.

Satan's arsenal consists of such things as fear, worry, doubt, and self-pity. Every one of these weapons robs us of peace and leaves us troubled inside. Do you want to discern where the enemy is coming against you? In the network of your relationships, wherever you do not have peace, you have war. Conversely, wherever you have peace, you have victory. When Satan hurls his darts against you, the more peace you have during adversity, the more truly you are walking in Christ's victory.

FRANCIS FRANGIPANE

# Following Him

# Lead On

*He guides me along the
right paths for his name's sake.*
PSALM 23:3 NIV

*E*ver heard the expression "taking the bit in your teeth"? A bit is a mouthpiece used to control a horse's movements. It is normally fitted so pressure on the reins presses the bit against the soft parts of the horse's mouth, causing it to turn its head. This expression alludes to a horse biting on the bit and taking control away from the rider, the one who should be in control.

How often we take the bit and wrestle control away from the Lord. Trying to do it *our* way. And as one pastor recently said, "How's that working for you?" Not always wonderfully well. The Interpreter's Bible says of this verse: "The straight path is not always the easiest; round about you may wander. . .while the straight path is through the defile, a dark and dangerous way. Nevertheless it is the road to be taken. To take easier journeys would mean you would be overtaken by the night before the sheepfold could be reached."

Our heavenly Father, who made the heavens and the earth, knows what He has planned for us. When we relinquish control and follow Him, allowing Him to guide us along the right path, we will have an easier time in our walk—not easy, but easier. For we can know without a doubt He has our best interests at heart. Following means staying behind the leader. Allow Him to guide you this day.

*Let the wise listen and add to their learning, and let the discerning get guidance.*

PROVERBS 1:5 NIV

---

*Have you ever come on anything quite like this extravagant generosity of God, this deep, deep wisdom? It's way over our heads. We'll never figure it out.*

ROMANS 11:33 MSG

---

*Then he said to them all: "Whoever wants to be my disciple must deny themselves and take up their cross daily and follow me. For whoever wants to save their life will lose it, but whoever loses their life for me will save it."*

LUKE 9:23–24 NIV

# Provide the Light

Dear Lord, how we long for You to show us the right path for our lives.
Please lead and guide us along the narrow way. Shine Your light before
us to keep us from stumbling. Draw us close to You and encourage us.
Your Word says You have plans for us and we want to follow them with
Your road map. Thank You, Father, for this exciting journey. Amen.

*"Follow me and I'll show you how. Self-help is no help at all. Self-sacrifice is the way, my way, to finding yourself, your true self. What kind of deal is it to get everything you want but lose yourself? What could you ever trade your soul for?"*

MATTHEW 16:25–26 MSG

---

*The clouds churn about at his direction. They do whatever he commands throughout the earth.*

JOB 37:12 NLT

---

*Do not be like the horse or the mule, which have no understanding but must be controlled by bit and bridle or they will not come to you.*

PSALM 32:9 NIV

The Christian life is a life that
consists of following Jesus.
A. W. PINK

It is Christ who is to be exalted, not
our feelings. We will know Him by
obedience, not by emotions. Our
love will be shown by obedience, not
by how good we feel about God at
a given moment. "And love means
following the commands of God." "Do
you love Me?" Jesus asked Peter. "Feed
My lambs." He was not asking, "How
do you feel about Me?" for love is not
a feeling. He was asking for action.
ELISABETH ELLIOT

*The LORD says, "I will guide you along
the best pathway for your life. I will
advise you and watch over you."*
PSALM 32:8 NLT

———⚬———

*I*f you're on a safari, a knowledgeable guide will lead you to the best vantage
point to see wildlife, educate you on what you're seeing, and protect you from
danger. God is like a safari guide who never leaves your side. He knows both the
joys and the dangers that surround you. Through His Spirit and scripture, God
will guide you toward a life of wonder and adventure. Stay close to His side and
allow Him to lead.

# In Your Care

Father God, You know how weak we are as we strive to follow You. Show us striving isn't the answer, but listening to the Holy Spirit is. Sharpen our ears to Your voice, so we hear the Shepherd's call. Teach us to trust in the way You would have us go, and forgive us when we grumble about the trip. Amen.

*So, my very dear friends, when you see people reducing God to something they can use or control, get out of their company as fast as you can.*

1 CORINTHIANS 10:14 MSG

———✦———

*"Return home, you wayward children," says the LORD, "for I am your master. I will bring you back to the land of Israel—one from this town and two from that family—from wherever you are scattered. And I will give you shepherds after my own heart, who will guide you with knowledge and understanding."*

JEREMIAH 3:14–15 NLT

How true it is that without the guidance of the Holy Spirit intellect not only is undependable but also extremely dangerous, because it often confuses the issue of right and wrong.

WATCHMAN NEE

After a hard day scrambling to find your way around in the world, it's assuring to come home to a place you know. God can be equally familiar to you. With time you can learn where to go for nourishment, where to hide for protection, where to turn for guidance. Just as your earthly house is a place of refuge, so God's house is a place of peace.

MAX LUCADO

Jesus said, "I am the Bread of Life. The person who aligns with me hungers no more and thirsts no more, ever. I have told you this explicitly because even though you have seen me in action, you don't really believe me. Every person the Father gives me eventually comes running to me. And once that person is with me, I hold on and don't let go. I came down from heaven not to follow my own whim but to accomplish the will of the One who sent me."

JOHN 6:35 MSG

# Protecting
# His Own

# Watching Out for Us

*Your rod and your staff
protect and comfort me.*
PSALM 23:4.NLT

In days of old, shepherds dug up saplings and carved them into rods until they became extensions of their hand. A young shepherd would practice for hours, learning to throw the rod accurately before he went out with the flock. A shepherd's rod served many purposes; it was most certainly the safeguard for the shepherd and his sheep, coming between them and any predator. But it also served as a tool for disciplining and correcting wayward sheep.

The staff also had another use. Phillip Keller writes, "Whereas the rod conveys the concept of authority, of power, of discipline, of defense against danger, the word *staff* speaks of all that is longsuffering and kind." A shepherd would use the crook on the staff to draw an individual sheep closer for examination and care. Or to capture an animal entangled in briars or too close to the edge of a cliff. He gently guided his animals, applying pressure to their sides with the end of the staff. The staff symbolizes all the gentle disciplines that help us through the darkest of times.

Our Lord and Savior applies the rod of discipline with the Holy Spirit. He is there to convict our hearts and allow us to repent from wrongdoing, then how quickly the Father forgives His sheep! Next He guides and comforts us with His staff, His presence. Our awesome Shepherd continually watches and protects His flock.

*"My God is my rock, in whom I find protection. He is my shield, the power that saves me, and my place of safety. He is my refuge, my savior, the one who saves me from violence."*

2 SAMUEL 22:3 NLT

---

*These things I remember as I pour out my soul: how I used to go to the house of God under the protection of the Mighty One with shouts of joy and praise among the festive throng.*

PSALM 42:4 NIV

---

*GOD's name is a place of protection— good people can run there and be safe.*

PROVERBS 18:10 MSG

My life is a mystery which I do
not attempt to really understand,
as though I were led by the hand
in a night where I see nothing,
but can fully depend on the love and
protection of Him who guides me.

THOMAS MERTON

The safest place in all the world
is in the will of God, and the
safest protection in all the
world is the name of God.

WARREN WIERSBE

*The angel of the LORD encamps around
those who fear him, and he delivers them.*

PSALM 34:7 NIV

———————

*I*n the Bible we read about angelic beings who act as God's messengers and
warriors. Far from cute little cherubs who do nothing more than pluck harps on
cotton-ball clouds, we meet angels who yield swords and have ferocious lion-like
faces. But the message they continually tell God's children is, "Be not afraid." When
you're in need of protection, remember there's more going on than is visible to the
eye. God's angels have your back.

# Time after Time

Father God, how blessed we are and we don't even realize it. You keep us from the precipice time after time. Your rod of discipline teaches us the way in which we should walk, keeping us on the narrow road. Once we realize our need for repentance and turn to You, forgiveness is extended and we feel the staff applied gently by the Spirit to keep us safe. How merciful You are. Thank You for Your loving-kindness. Amen.

*But let all who take refuge in you be glad;*
*let them ever sing for joy. Spread your*
*protection over them, that those who*
*love your name may rejoice in you.*

PSALM 5:11 NIV

---

*"God's way is perfect. All the LORD's*
*promises prove true. He is a shield for*
*all who look to him for protection.*
*For who is God except the LORD?*
*Who but our God is a solid rock?"*

2 SAMUEL 22:31–32 NLT

---

*Trust GOD from the bottom of your heart;*
*don't try to figure out everything on your*
*own. Listen for GOD's voice in everything*
*you do, everywhere you go; he's the one*
*who will keep you on track. Don't assume*
*that you know it all. Run to GOD! Run*
*from evil! Your body will glow with*
*health, your very bones will vibrate with*
*life! Honor GOD with everything you*
*own; give him the first and the best. Your*
*barns will burst, your wine vats will brim*
*over. But don't, dear friend, resent GOD's*
*discipline; don't sulk under his loving*
*correction. It's the child he loves that GOD*
*corrects; a father's delight is behind all this.*

PROVERBS 3:5–12 MSG

*Blessed are those whose strength is in you,*
*whose hearts are set on pilgrimage.*

PSALM 84:5 NIV

———— ◦ ————

ou're embarking on a lifelong spiritual journey. It's a pilgrimage that will follow a different path from that of anyone else who has ever desired to grow closer to God. The prayers you pray, how quickly you mature, the battles you fight, the challenges you overcome, and the person you become will all add up to a one-of-a-kind adventure. Look to God instead of comparing yourself to others to gauge how far you've come and what direction you're headed next.

# Our Shepherd

Heavenly Father, we sheep need Your ever-present help. The road and byways become so muddled at times, it's hard to figure out where we should step. Keep us in Your sights, tapping us on the shoulder with Your staff, letting us feel Your very presence when we need You. Our hearts are filled with expectations of what lies beyond, because we know You are guiding and directing our steps. Amen.

*The LORD knows people's thoughts;*
*he knows they are worthless! Joyful are*
*those you discipline, LORD, those you teach*
*with your instructions. You give them*
*relief from troubled times until a pit is*
*dug to capture the wicked.*

PSALM 94:11–13 NLT

---

*For the kingdom of God is not a*
*matter of talk but of power. What do*
*you prefer? Shall I come to you with*
*a rod of discipline, or shall I come in*
*love and with a gentle spirit?*

1 CORINTHIANS 4:20–21 NIV

We often learn more of God under
the rod that strikes us than under
the staff that comforts us.

STEPHEN CHARNOCK

In the destiny of every moral being
there is an object more worthy of God
than happiness. It is character. And
the grand aim of man's creation is the
development of a grand character, and
grand character is, by its very nature,
the product of probationary discipline.

AUSTIN PHELPS

*"So, my dear friends, listen carefully;
those who embrace these my ways
are most blessed. Mark a life of discipline
and live wisely; don't squander your
precious life. Blessed the man, blessed the
woman, who listens to me, awake and
ready for me each morning, alert and
responsive as I start my day's work. When
you find me, you find life, real life, to say
nothing of GOD's good pleasure."*
PROVERBS 8:32–35 MSG

> *For this reason I remind you to fan into flame the gift of God, which is in you through the laying on of my hands. For the Spirit God gave us does not make us timid, but gives us power, love and self-discipline.*
>
> 2 TIMOTHY 1:6–7 NIV

# In the Midst

# Fearful Times

*You prepare a table before me*
*in the presence of my enemies.*
PSALM 23:5 NIV

Stormy weather. Trials and tribulations. Worry and anxiety. Let's fret.

When these thoughts overtake us, it's easy to fall into the well of self-pity. Where is God when we need Him? Doesn't He see what's going on? Yes. He does. And He isn't taken by surprise. In fact, He's prepared a feast, a celebration—what? He is celebrating my trials and tribulations? Yes, because when we are weak, His strength is magnified.

Now is the time to make a choice to praise Him and rejoice. It's not easy, but changing our focus alleviates much of the stress we take on. During World War II, when the bombing was at its worst, this verse was a well-used text for sermons. It drove home the point of relying on His strength to get through tough times.

When we look at this verse, we see that in the midst of our "enemies"—Satan and his crew—He is taking care of us abundantly. Despite our groveling, He extends His hand of mercy and love. Our divine Host exceeds the basic hospitality just for us, and our enemy slinks away because we are a guest under His protection. How can we worry when we know that?

Choose today to change your perspective and concentrate on His goodness. Thank Him—for He's the Greatest Host of all.

....................................................

....................................................

....................................................

....................................................

....................................................

....................................................

....................................................

....................................................

....................................................

....................................................

....................................................

....................................................

*We who have run for our very lives to God have every reason to grab the promised hope with both hands and never let go. It's an unbreakable spiritual lifeline, reaching past all appearances right to the very presence of God.*

HEBREWS 6:18–20 MSG

---

*Worry weighs a person down.*

PROVERBS 12:25 NLT

---

*GOD is all strength for his people, ample refuge for his chosen leader; Save your people and bless your heritage. Care for them; carry them like a good shepherd.*

PSALM 28:8–9 MSG

Begin to rejoice in the Lord, and your bones will flourish like an herb, and your cheeks will glow with the bloom of health and freshness. Worry, fear, distrust, care—all are poisonous! Joy is balm and healing, and if you will but rejoice, God will give power.

A. B. Simpson

―――――・◦・―――――

The branch of the vine does not worry, and toil, and rush here to seek for sunshine, and there to find rain. No; it rests in union and communion with the vine; and at the right time, and in the right way, is the right fruit found on it. Let us so abide in the Lord Jesus.

Hudson Taylor

*Stay with GOD! Take heart. Don't quit.*
*I'll say it again: Stay with GOD.*
PSALM 27:14 MSG

———— • ————

ife is short, but some days seem to last forever. When you're facing a difficult day, don't face it alone. Take a good look at your exhaustion, anxiety, and fears. Picture entrusting them, one-by-one, into God's hands. Then take an objective look at what you need to do today. Invite God to join you as you take one step at a time in accomplishing what lies ahead. Throughout the day, remind yourself that God is right by your side.

# Uncertainty

Father God, life circumstances have thrown us, and we are on shaky ground. Our knees tremble and our hearts quake. Let us feel Your very presence at this time. Do not let fear overtake us; keep us strong. We turn to Your Word and read David's words knowing despite the presence of our enemies, You are beside us. Reach out a hand of mercy and calm our fears. Amen.

*"That is why I tell you not to worry about everyday life—whether you have enough food and drink, or enough clothes to wear."*
MATTHEW 6:25 NLT

---

*"Who of you by worrying can add a single hour to your life?"*
LUKE 12:25 NIV

---

*"But blessed is the man who trusts me, GOD, the woman who sticks with GOD. They're like trees replanted in Eden, putting down roots near the rivers— Never a worry through the hottest of summers, never dropping a leaf, serene and calm through droughts, bearing fresh fruit every season."*
JEREMIAH 17:7–8 MSG

What is needed for happy effectual service is simply to put your work into the Lord's hand, and leave it there. Do not take it to Him in prayer, saying, "Lord, guide me, Lord, give me wisdom, Lord, arrange for me," and then arise from your knees, and take the burden all back, and try to guide and arrange for yourself. Leave it with the Lord, and remember that what you trust to Him you must not worry over nor feel anxious about. Trust and worry cannot go together.

HANNAH WHITALL SMITH

*They will have no fear of bad news;*
*their hearts are steadfast, trusting in the LORD.*
PSALM 112:7 NIV

The fear of bad news is what worry is all about. Trusting God is what makes that fear fade away. So the next time fear begins tugging at your heart, turn every worry that's weighing you down into a prayer. The more this becomes habit, the more you'll notice your perspective beginning to change. You'll start to anticipate seeing God bring something good out of any and every situation. For God, even bad news is an opportunity to work miracles.

# Leaning In

Dear heavenly Father, thank You for loving us despite our unloveliness. We ask You to forgive us for grumbling and hear instead our praise. The situations before us look bleak and gloomy, yet we choose to lift our hearts and voices and to say thank You for all You have done in our lives. We lean on You to show us the next step. Trusting in Your Word, we wait and hope. Amen.

*Humble yourselves, therefore, under
God's mighty hand, that he may
lift you up in due time. Cast all your
anxiety on him because he cares for you.*

1 PETER 5:6–7 NIV

---

*"And if God cares so wonderfully for
wildflowers that are here today and
thrown into the fire tomorrow, he will
certainly care for you. Why do you have
so little faith? So don't worry about these
things, saying, 'What will we eat? What
will we drink? What will we wear?'"*

MATTHEW 6:30–31 NLT

---

*"How great the glory of GOD!"
And here's why: GOD, high above,
sees far below; no matter the distance,
he knows everything about us.*

PSALM 138:5–6 MSG

# Home at Last

# Journey's End

*I'm back home in the house*
*of* GOD *for the rest of my life.*
PSALM 23:6 MSG

t the end of the journey, the tired sheep are led into the fold, a place of safety and rest. The shepherd has done his job and delivered them home. So it is with a believer: at the end of our journey, we go home.

Not every person has the luxury of coming from a peaceful home: fireplace roaring, laughter filling the rooms, joyful hosts. However, believers have hope because they know they have a home—and as the psalmist wrote—for the rest of their life. The divine Host has readied a place for us and it is to this end we must shift our focus. It might be many years until we go to the mansion He has prepared, but until that time, we can know without a shadow of a doubt it's waiting, built and ready.

William R. Taylor states, "The end of the God-guided life, as portrayed in scripture, is extraordinarily splendid, and we should not be afraid of dealing with it." For at that time, we will be in His presence. Forever. Even though we have our good days and bad days, the Lord will see us through it all. For the Lord is good and His mercy endures forever.

*"Where, O death, is your victory?
Where, O death, is your sting?"*

1 Corinthians 15:55 NIV

---

*So we don't look at the troubles we can
see now; rather, we fix our gaze on
things that cannot be seen. For the things
we see now will soon be gone, but the
things we cannot see will last forever.*

2 Corinthians 4:18 NLT

---

*But here on this mountain,
God-of-the-Angel-Armies. . . He'll
banish death forever. And God will wipe
the tears from every face. He'll remove
every sign of disgrace from his people,
wherever they are. Yes! God says so!*

Isaiah 25:7–9 MSG

When the time comes for you to die, you need not be afraid, because death cannot separate you from God's love.

CHARLES SPURGEON

———

I am so glad God will never allow a man to go comfortably and peacefully to eternal death. He never allows any man to be lost until He has done His best to save him.

CLOVIS G. CHAPPELL

———

Death may be the king of terrors. . . but Jesus is the King of kings!

D. L. MOODY

*Be brave. Be strong. Don't give up.*
*Expect GOD to get here soon*
PSALM 31:24 MSG

———————◆◆———————

*T*rusting God can help transform you into a "glass half full" kind of person. You can face every day, even the tough ones, with confidence and expectation because you're aware there's more to life than can be seen. You can rest in the promise that God is working all things together for your good. You know death is not the end. In other words, you can expect that great things lie ahead. Why not anticipate them with thanks and praise?

# You Are Faithful

Dear heavenly Father, how grateful we are that You have walked us through the valleys and the shadows, never losing hold of our hands. Keep us on Your pathway, Lord, until the end of our lives, so we might dwell in Your Kingdom forever. Help us to trust in You for Your perfect peace, no matter what. We love You and choose to stay close in the fold. Amen.

_But you have come to Mount Zion, to the city of the living God, the heavenly Jerusalem. You have come to thousands upon thousands of angels in joyful assembly, to the church of the firstborn, whose names are written in heaven. You have come to God, the Judge of all, to the spirits of the righteous made perfect, to Jesus the mediator of a new covenant, and to the sprinkled blood that speaks a better word than the blood of Abel._

HEBREWS 12:22–24 NIV

We want to reach the kingdom of God, but we don't want to travel by way of death. And yet there stands necessity saying: "This way, please." Do not hesitate, man, to go this way, when this is the way that God came to you.

SAINT AUGUSTINE

God shapes the world by prayer. Prayers are deathless. The lips that uttered them may be closed to death, the heart that felt them may have ceased to beat, but the prayers live before God, and God's heart is set on them and prayers outlive the lives of those who uttered them; they outlive a generation, outlive an age, outlive a world.

E. M. BOUNDS

*My health may fail, and my spirit may
grow weak, but God remains the strength
of my heart; he is mine forever.*
PSALM 73:26 NLT

your body is amazingly resilient, yet terminally fragile. Fashioned by God's lovingly creative hand, it was not designed to last. But you were. That's because you are so much more than your body. But God cares about all of you, your body and your soul. Even if your health fails, He will not. He is near. He hears every prayer, even those you hesitate to pray. Call on Him. His hope and healing reach beyond this life into the next.

# Grateful Hearts

Father God, our hearts are filled with praise and wonder. You have done so much for us and for that we are ever grateful. Give us mercy and grace to face the shadows and valleys, knowing You are with us every step we make. At the end of life's journey, when it's time for us to move into the mansion You have built, hold us close, so we might feel Your heartbeat. Amen.

But let the godly rejoice. Let them be glad in God's presence. Let them be filled with joy. Sing praises to God and to his name! Sing loud praises to him who rides the clouds. His name is the LORD— rejoice in his presence!

PSALM 68:3–4 NLT

---

And he said, "These are they who have come out of the great tribulation; they have washed their robes and made them white in the blood of the Lamb. Therefore, they are before the throne of God and serve him day and night in his temple; and he who sits on the throne will shelter them with his presence. 'Never again will they hunger; never again will they thirst. The sun will not beat down on them,' nor any scorching heat."

REVELATION 7:14–16 NIV

In His Service

# Serving Him

*You honor me by anointing*
*my head with oil.*
PSALM 23:5 NLT

*W*eary from the journey, the traveler came to the table prepared for him and found not only a feast but someone willing to welcome him further. To anoint with oil is not an image that means much to us, but in David's time it was a well-known custom. It was also routine in hot climates to mix the oil with perfume, which gave it a stimulating sensation thus providing a means of refreshment for exhausted travelers. The oil was also curative for many aches and pains. After receiving the oil, the recipient was invigorated and better fitted for action. Truly it was an appreciated practice.

In Psalm 23, the Host has gone the second mile in giving all that is required for renewing power and providing comfort. No point of hospitality was ignored. God rejuvenated the soul and spirit, making the heir ready for action.

Today He has provided us with the Holy Spirit, whom the oil symbolizes, to make us fit to travel the pathway on which we should serve. We are ready now to follow Him and run the race in the way He directs. Along the way we sing a song penned by James Edward Seddon, "Go forth and tell! O Church of God awake! God's saving news to all the nations take!"

*So we keep on praying for you, asking our God to enable you to live a life worthy of his call. May he give you the power to accomplish all the good things your faith prompts you to do. Then the name of our Lord Jesus will be honored because of the way you live, and you will be honored along with him. This is all made possible because of the grace of our God and Lord, Jesus Christ.*

2 Thessalonians 1:11–12 nlt

All Christians are but God's stewards.
Everything we have is on loan
from the Lord, entrusted to us for
a while to use in serving Him.

JOHN MACARTHUR

---

Whatever man may stand, whatever
he may do, to whatever he may
apply his hand—in agriculture,
in commerce, and in industry, or
his mind, in the world of art and
science—he is, in whatsoever it may
be, constantly standing before the face
of God. He is employed in the service
of his God. He has strictly to obey his
God. And above all, he has to aim
at the glory of his God.

ABRAHAM KUYPER

*I cry out to God Most High,*
*to God, who vindicates me.*
PSALM 57:2 NIV

———•◦•———

A beautiful woman like yourself was created for more than decoration. You were created for a purpose. Your purpose is not a specific job God has designated for you to accomplish. It's more like a unique spot He's designed for you to fill. God is working with you, encouraging you to grow into this "sweet spot." As you learn to lean on Him, God will help you discover the true joy and significance that come from simply being "you."

# Use Us

Father God, bless Your holy name. We want to follow Your paths and serve You all of our days. Send forth Your Holy Spirit unto our hearts so we might be of use in Your kingdom. Teach us and guide us for a right fit, a place of advantage, that we might give so others will benefit. Thank You, Lord, for all You have done for us. Amen.

*Therefore I glory in Christ Jesus in my service to God. I will not venture to speak of anything except what Christ has accomplished through me.*

ROMANS 15:17–18 NIV

———•———

*If anyone speaks, they should do so as one who speaks the very words of God. If anyone serves, they should do so with the strength God provides, so that in all things God may be praised through Jesus Christ. To him be the glory and the power for ever and ever. Amen.*

1 PETER 4:11 NIV

The highest form of worship is the worship of unselfish Christian service.

BILLY GRAHAM

We cannot all go to the foreign field.
We must express our interest in those
who have not had our opportunities
by our gifts. Much of the service
we render in our own land must be
rendered in the same way. But when
that is said, the fact still remains that
there is nothing that will take the place
of our hand-to-hand dealing with
those who need us. We cannot perform
all our charities by proxy. We must
come in personal contact with those
whom we would help.

CLOVIS G. CHAPPELL

*Serve the LORD with gladness;*
*Come before His presence with singing.*
PSALM 100:2 NKJV

We live in a needy world. People around the globe need food and medical care. People in our city need shelter. Our church needs volunteers to serve in the nursery. We can't fill every need. And God doesn't expect us to. We have limited time, energy, and resources. That's why prayer is such an important part of serving. Only with God's help will we have the wisdom and courage to say yes or no to the opportunities.

# Here We Are

Dear heavenly Father, our feet are shod with the truths from Your Word. We are armed and ready to go, following the Holy Spirit in action. Let our mouths be full of words of life to tell others of Your great goodness and mercy. Show us where You would have us go. We want to be of service to the Kingdom. Amen.

*So let's not allow ourselves to get fatigued doing good. At the right time we will harvest a good crop if we don't give up, or quit. Right now, therefore, every time we get the chance, let us work for the benefit of all, starting with the people closest to us in the community of faith.*

GALATIANS 6:9–10 MSG

*And now, dear brothers and sisters, one final thing. Fix your thoughts on what is true, and honorable, and right, and pure, and lovely, and admirable. Think about things that are excellent and worthy of praise. Keep putting into practice all you learned and received from me—everything you heard from me and saw me doing. Then the God of peace will be with you.*

PHILIPPIANS 4:8–9 NLT

# Blessed Beyond Measure

*My cup brims with blessing.*

PSALM 23:5 MSG

Have you ever felt your heart so full of gratitude you thought it might explode? Imagine the psalmist in this portion of scripture. He's hiding from his enemies. The Host has provided him with a feast, care for his body, and a hiding place. At this point in time, he realizes how blessed he is—not just a little bit, but a cup brimming with goodness. He focuses on that very moment. Not what's coming next, but the present.

Oh, that we would learn to do that very thing. To focus on the here and now and what good things the Lord has brought us to. We might have walked through valleys, dodged arrows, but at this moment in time, we rose from slumber, drew in a deep breath, and now can rest and rejoice knowing full well the Lord is beside us. He cares. He loves. He provides. He has given us the Holy Spirit, the Comforter as that extra measure of blessing.

Thankfulness is a learned attitude, one you must practice daily. Our thoughts can be swayed quickly by circumstances, and as real as those are, if we have practiced our gratefulness lesson, we can still rejoice in recognition of all the things the Lord has done for us. Choose to be grateful today, for you are blessed.

*How abundant are the good things that you have stored up for those who fear you, that you bestow in the sight of all, on those who take refuge in you.*

PSALM 31:19 NIV

———◆———

*Since we are receiving a Kingdom that is unshakable, let us be thankful and please God by worshiping him with holy fear and awe.*

HEBREWS 12:28 NLT

———◆———

*Hannah prayed: I'm bursting with GOD-news! I'm walking on air.*

1 SAMUEL 2:1 MSG

He had not only a fullness of abundance, but of redundance. Those that have this happiness must carry their cup upright and see that it overflows into their poor brethren's emptier vessels.

JOHN TRAPP

My cup runneth over—it is not merely "full"; it runs over. This, too, indicates abundance; and from the abundance of the favors thus bestowed, the psalmist infers that God would always provide for him, and that He would never leave him to want.

JOHN BARNES

*You will eat the fruit of your labor;*
*blessings and prosperity will be yours.*
PSALM 128:2 NIV

———————•◦•———————

*S*ome blessings are ours simply because God loves us. Other blessings come as a result of working with God. When it's within our ability, God expects us to play an active role in answering our own prayers. We pray for provision, yet continue to perform faithfully at work. We pray for better marriages, yet do our part to love and forgive. We pray for better health, yet watch what we eat. Between our labor and God's love, we're doubly blessed.

# Thankful Hearts

Dear heavenly Father, how we love You. Thank You for all the blessings You have provided by Your hand. It is inconceivable to us that You sent Your Son, that You redeemed us, that You love us so much to cast away our sins. Our attitude is one of thanksgiving and praise all of our days. For we know, Father, Your goodness is overwhelming. We love You, Lord. Amen.

*"Starting with Samuel, every prophet spoke about what is happening today. You are the children of those prophets, and you are included in the covenant God promised to your ancestors. For God said to Abraham, 'Through your descendants all the families on earth will be blessed.' When God raised up his servant, Jesus, he sent him first to you people of Israel, to bless you by turning each of you back from your sinful ways."*

ACTS 3:24–26 NLT

———◆———

*Blessed is the one who always trembles before God.*

PROVERBS 28:14 NIV

Worship is giving God the best that He has given you. Be careful what you do with the best you have. Whenever you get a blessing from God, give it back to Him as a love gift. Take time to meditate before God and offer the blessing back to Him in a deliberate act of worship. If you hoard a thing for yourself, it will turn into spiritual dry rot, as the manna did when it was hoarded. God will never let you hold a spiritual thing for yourself; it has to be given back to Him that He may make it a blessing to others.

OSWALD CHAMBERS

*Now I'm alert to GOD's ways;*
*I don't take God for granted.*
PSALM 18:21 MSG

———————◆———————

The phrase "Thank God!" has lost much of its meaning these days. People use it interchangeably with expressions such as "Wow!", "Thank goodness!", or "I really lucked out!" That's because people feel a surge of gratitude when good things happen to them, but not all of them are certain where they should direct their thanks. You've caught a glimpse of God's goodness. You know who is behind the blessings you receive. Don't hesitate to say, "Thank God!"

# We Are Wowed

Dearest Lord Jesus, we lift our hearts and minds full of gratitude to say thank You for Your goodness. We do not wonder from whom all good gifts come, for we know the Gift-bearer. You have given beyond measure to these humble sheep and our thankfulness knows no bounds. We lift our voices to sing Your praises. Blessed we are—because of You. Amen.

........................................................................................
........................................................................................
........................................................................................
........................................................................................
........................................................................................
........................................................................................
........................................................................................
........................................................................................
........................................................................................
........................................................................................
........................................................................................
........................................................................................
........................................................................................
........................................................................................
........................................................................................

"But blessed is the one who trusts in
the LORD, whose confidence is in him.
They will be like a tree planted by the
water that sends out its roots by the
stream. It does not fear when heat
comes; its leaves are always green.
It has no worries in a year of drought
and never fails to bear fruit."

JEREMIAH 17:7–8 NIV

Blessed is the one who does not walk in
step with the wicked or stand in the way
that sinners take or sit in the company of
mockers, but whose delight is in the law
of the LORD, and who meditates on his
law day and night. That person is like a
tree planted by streams of water.

PSALM 1:1–3 NIV

Be Happy

# Thrilling News

*Your beauty and love chase after me.*
PSALM 23:6 MSG

God chases after us? Aren't we to reach out to Him and ask for the pathway to happiness? Oh, my friend. Our loving God chases after us. He wants our hearts and lives! God wants us to be happy. And happiness is found in following Jesus. We often take our own paths, choosing ways that aren't pleasing to Him, and then we're tangled in briars and brambles. Joy and happiness are more easily found when we pursue what He has intended for our lives and are obedient to His Word.

Happiness is touted in advertising. We're bombarded with the thought that we deserve happiness. The word *deserve* is synonymous with merit, being worthy of. Are we worthy of happiness? Only through the blood of Christ after we relinquish our hold on our lives to the Lord and choose to walk in His light.

Peter wrote: "Though you have not seen him, you love him; and even though you do not see him now, you believe in him and are filled with an inexpressible and glorious joy" (1 Peter 1:8 NIV). That's how our hearts will feel when we totally surrender our lives to Jesus. Resting in faith that He is working for our good, we can be joyful! Be happy!

............................................

............................................

............................................

............................................

............................................

............................................

............................................

............................................

............................................

............................................

............................................

............................................

............................................

............................................

............................................

*"The LORD, the LORD himself, is my strength and my defense; he has become my salvation." With joy you will draw water from the wells of salvation.*

ISAIAH 12:2–3 NIV

———❖———

*Yet I will rejoice in the LORD,
I will be joyful in God my Savior.*

HABAKKUK 3:18 NIV

———❖———

*It's what God does with your life as he sets it right, puts it together, and completes it with joy.*

ROMANS 14:17 MSG

............................................

............................................

............................................

............................................

............................................

............................................

............................................

............................................

............................................

............................................

............................................

Let us remember the loving-kindness of the Lord and rehearse His deeds of grace. Let us open the volume of recollection, which is so richly illuminated with memories of His mercy, and we will soon be happy.

ALISTAIR BEGG

———————

There is a joy which is not given to the ungodly, but to those who love Thee for Thine own sake, whose joy Thou Thyself art. And this is the happy life, to rejoice to Thee, of Thee, for Thee; this it is, and there is no other.

SAINT AUGUSTINE

*Live a happy life! Keep your eyes
open for GOD, watch for his works;
be alert for signs of his presence.*
PSALM 105:3–4 MSG

———·◦·———

*B*abies often smile when they catch sight of their mother's face. Catching a glimpse of God can do the same for us. It can make our hearts happy. Yet God's presence is much more subtle than that of a human parent. God reveals Himself in quiet ways, such as in an answer to prayer, the glory of a sunset, or the gift of a new friend. Keep your eyes open. God is ever present and at work in your life.

# Overjoyed

Father God, our hearts burst with happiness when we recount the ways You have blessed and kept us. An attitude of gratitude paints our lives and gives us such contentment. When we focus on You and Your Word, life's circumstances pale in comparison to Your glory. Thank You for all You have done for us. Amen.

> *"Sing praise-songs to GOD. He's done it all! Let the whole earth know what he's done! Raise the roof! Sing your hearts out, O Zion! The Greatest lives among you: The Holy of Israel."*
>
> ISAIAH 12:5–6 MSG

---

> *May the God of hope fill you with all joy and peace as you trust in him, so that you may overflow with hope by the power of the Holy Spirit.*
>
> ROMANS 15:13 NIV

If man is not made for God,
why is he happy only in God?

BLAISE PASCAL

———————•❖•———————

God will prepare everything for
our perfect happiness in heaven,
and if it takes my dog being there,
I believe he'll be there.

BILLY GRAHAM

———————•❖•———————

Our purpose should be to discover
the gifts He has given us and to use
those gifts faithfully and joyfully in
His service, without either envying or
disparaging the gifts we do not have.

JOHN MACARTHUR

> *"Only you are my Lord! Every good
> thing I have is a gift from you."*
> PSALM 16:2 CEV

———•◦•———

What is good about your life? Consider how every good thing we receive can be tied back to God. Family. Friends. Talents. The ability to earn an income. It's easy to take the good things in our lives for granted while readily putting the blame on God when we feel things go wrong. The next time you notice you're feeling happy about something good in your life, look for the part God played in sending it your way.

....................................................................................

....................................................................................

....................................................................................

....................................................................................

....................................................................................

....................................................................................

....................................................................................

....................................................................................

....................................................................................

....................................................................................

....................................................................................

....................................................................................

....................................................................................

....................................................................................

....................................................................................

# Our Worthy God

Dearest Lord, thank You for reaching down from heaven and capturing our hearts. We know we do not deserve Your loving-kindness. It is by Your mercy and goodness we have our salvation. You gave the Greatest Gift. Bless Your Holy Name. You are most worthy of praise and worship. These sheep choose to follow, and we will walk in Your pathways forever. Amen.

*Shout joyful praises to God, all the earth!
Sing about the glory of his name! Tell the
world how glorious he is. Say to God,
"How awesome are your deeds! Your
enemies cringe before your mighty power."*

PSALM 66:1–3 NLT

---

*I will give thanks to you, LORD,
with all my heart; I will tell of all
your wonderful deeds. I will be glad
and rejoice in you; I will sing the
praises of your name, O Most High.*

PSALM 9:1–2 NIV

All in All

# My Everything

*The LORD is my shepherd,*
*I have all that I need.*
PSALM 23:1 NLT

———— ·◦· ————

*N*eed and want. Two words we bandy about when we consider our lives. We need. . .we want. If you watch television for thirty minutes, you'll be subjected to at least five minutes of what you want, be it a new car or dish detergent that is gentle on the hands. It's easy to get caught up in that mind-set—and find it can be dangerous to the wallet.

Scripture tells us if we rest in Him, we will have all we need. Psalm 23 depicts the Lord as a shepherd. Should several flocks come together, a sheep will lift its head at the sound of his master's voice. He knows that particular person who takes care of him and so he follows obediently to find food and water and shelter. A shepherd takes great care of each animal for he knows its value.

So the Lord knows our value. He made us. Created us to give Him glory and honor.

The Interpreter's Bible states: "Only so one can say the Lord is my shepherd; only so can one be confident I shall not want." When we choose Him, He is our Provider and Friend. Our Good Shepherd. Our All in all.

In the midst of the awesomeness, a touch comes, and you know it is the right hand of Jesus Christ. You know it is not the hand of restraint, correction, nor chastisement, but the right hand of the Everlasting Father. Whenever His hand is laid upon you, it gives inexpressible peace and comfort, and the sense that "underneath are the everlasting arms" (Deuteronomy 33:27), full of support, provision, comfort, and strength.

OSWALD CHAMBERS

Our need is not to prove God's faithfulness but to demonstrate our own, by trusting Him both to determine and to supply our needs according to His will.

JOHN MACARTHUR

# Forever Thankful

Heavenly Father, how do we express our gratitude? We are a wayward flock You brought into the fold. You have cleansed us and provided for us to the fullest measure. Our lives are a product of Your grace and mercy. "Thank You" cannot begin to describe how full our hearts are. Jesus paid it all. We surrender. Take our lives and help us live them for You. Amen.

*"What I'm trying to do here is get you to relax, not be so preoccupied with getting so you can respond to God's giving. People who don't know God and the way he works fuss over these things, but you know both God and how he works. Steep yourself in God-reality, God-initiative, God-provisions. You'll find all your everyday human concerns will be met. Don't be afraid of missing out. You're my dearest friends! The Father wants to give you the very kingdom itself."*

LUKE 12:29–32 MSG

Prayer is the open admission that
without Christ we can do nothing.
And prayer is the turning away from
ourselves to God in the confidence
that He will provide the help we need.
Prayer humbles us as needy and
exalts God as wealthy.

JOHN PIPER

———◆———

The hope that God has provided for
you is not merely a wish. Neither is it
dependent on other people, possessions,
or circumstances for its validity.
Instead, biblical hope is an application
of your faith that supplies a confident
expectation in God's fulfillment of
His promises. Coupled with faith
and love, hope is part of the abiding
characteristics in a believer's life.

JOHN BROGER

*Where morning dawns, where evening*
*fades, you call forth songs of joy.*
PSALM 65:8 NIV

―•―

*H*appiness is usually the result of circumstance. Joy, however, bubbles up unbidden, often persisting in spite of circumstance. It's an excitement that simmers below the surface, an assurance that God is working behind the scenes, a contentment that deepens as you discover your place in the world. The more at home you feel with God, the more joy will make a home in your heart—a welcome reminder that God is near.

# Amazing Grace

Father God, we rest in You. We traveled the hard road, and You found us. You led us through the narrow gate by Your Son and tucked us under Your wing to shelter us. We run to You for Your extravagant good gifts, which none of us deserve aside from Your Son's sacrifice. Help us keep our eyes on You until we join You in heaven. Amen.

*There is none like God. . .riding to*
*your rescue through the skies,*
*his dignity haloed by clouds.*

DEUTERONOMY 33:26 MSG

---

*"You are worthy, our Lord and God, to*
*receive glory and honor and power, for*
*you created all things, and by your will*
*they were created and have their being."*

REVELATION 4:11 NIV

*Great and mighty God, whose name is the LORD Almighty, great are your purposes and mighty are your deeds. Your eyes are open to the ways of all mankind; you reward each person according to their conduct and as their deeds deserve.*

JEREMIAH 32:18–19 NIV